# Skin

# Skin

Chris Jones

Longbarrow Press

Published in 2015 by
Longbarrow Press
76 Holme Lane
Sheffield
S6 4JW

www.longbarrowpress.com

Printed by T.J. International Ltd,
Padstow, Cornwall

Some of these poems, or versions of, have been
previously published in the following magazines and books,
to whose editors I am grateful:
*Five* (One Three Six Publishing, 1999)
*Miniatures* (Longbarrow Press, 2007)
*Staple* 72 (2009)
*The Forward Book of Poetry 2011*
*All Things Bright and Beautiful* (catalogue for exhibition
at 20-21 Visual Arts Centre, 2012)
*Jigs and Reels* (Shoestring Press, 2013)
*The Footing* (Longbarrow Press, 2013)
*Cambridge Primary English Learner's Book 5* (CUP, 2015)

ISBN 978-1-906175-25-2

First edition

# Contents

The painter saw what was, an alternate
Candour and secrecy inside the skin.

'In Santa Maria del Popolo', Thom Gunn

# Back

Last night I washed my father's back,
dreamed young again his hair was black

and his smooth skin was deeply tanned.
I cleaned him with my mother's hand.

(My sister stood beside his head,
my brother played away instead.)

On grass by fragmentary trees
my father crouched down on his knees

so I could wipe his back of sweat.
Our understanding: I forget.

# Skin

## 1

At thirteen my skinny body peeled apart.  My throat closed up,
cleft with ulcers; my mouth and tongue foamed and blistered.
The tip of my penis bubbled then scabbed over.

This was the month of blossom pinking trees, of schoolmates
necking by the fences; the month the ships pushed southward.

## 2

My skin, layers of skin, had separated.  And because my lungs
were tacked with phlegm, since I hadn't peed for days, the next
recourse was hospital.  I peered through the ambulance's tinted
doors; gazed from my isolated room at children hooked to
limpid bags and tubes.

I watched a TV screen that moved and moved with grey-green
sea.

## 3

I kept to a course of manageable things: lucent jars of Vaseline,
spittoons (a physio came to beat my back like skins), and cups
of medicine to light my throat.

One morning, medics crowded round the glass.  Two clinicians
pitched up to snap my eyes and mouth.  The black Sister who
wandered through my nights must have known, could have
recalled, some faraway island pummelled by storms.

4

When the young doctor breezed in to check my notes and said 'So many cards – lots of hugs and kisses?' I thought of an untouchable girl: lip-gloss and freckles. Everyone, it seemed, was dreaming of a sweetheart they'd left behind.


5

The sickness was leaving me, though one afternoon I started to yammer and wouldn't shut up. Maybe it was horses thump-circling on the box. Maybe it was the infection riddling everybody's blood, that springtime fever. Maybe it was because my scabs were crumbling, my rank mouth firming back into a mouth.


6

Just as my dermis and epidermis were melding back together, just as my sores were healing over, I watched men on TV being flayed by fire.

On board the *Coventry, Sheffield*, those who met the blasts must have crackled black. What footage showed were boats carrying the badly burnt; padded bandages making up large and useless hands: so much singed and weeping flesh. Blokes looked wide of everyone, amazed at how flimsy they'd become.

My thirteen-year-old self, scoured and picked as I was, could comprehend the body's vicissitudes, could gauge the absolute waste of skin.

# Sentences

For months on Tuesday afternoons
I'd swing and lock the three gates from staff room

to B wing, then linger, pick my lines of sight
beneath the nets and railings, Victorian light,

before sidling up to Alim on the ones
sweeping hair and skin of prisoners

in little piles; and here was me
bodied with trees, sun, asking 'where's your poetry?'

\*

A small, black handgun shut up Alim:
in a gloomy bar some crack-head shot at him.

Since this kid was an informer
police closed like a forest, flipped Alim's words over,

proffered rooms with thin daylight and deadening walls:
no visits, no shower, no telephone calls

until the arc of their story undercut his.
He almost hit a whisper telling me this.

\*

Alim's poems were packs of terriers
that yapped, turned tail and sniffed the air

for scents locked out beyond the fences;
clattered under mattresses,

clawed around cell doors and stairwells
hard on stale and sluggish smells.

His work played landings, was sold for burn
nailed prizes in the competition

which needled lifers writing heartfelt lines –
who was this guy hardly doing time,

who still had latch keys to his name,
could conjure the bleachy taste of rain

swaying on a ladder of his own words,
scaling the whitewashed prison walls?

*

There was that time Alim watched smoke
fray above his head, when he huddled and joked:

'I did not commit *this* crime', smuggling words
through twilight as men roared

across the wing.  Said: 'I miss Louise most
the moment she walks in – rain freckling her coat

and perfume twined around her wrists and throat;
lisping *Alim, no worries, you'll soon be out.*

Even as she bends there in the flesh
I play out how she'll slip the wire and mesh

past screws believing all their dirty knowledge,
dogs that sniff between her legs;

how she'll halt at the bus stop and gulp deep breaths
of sunshine, cry as she lights a cigarette.'

\*

I took Alim for a dealer, and asked him straight.
'Yeah, cunning aren't I?' Not a punt in the dark

for a savvy cleaner to be touting goods
to milky-eyed junkies in his neighbourhood.

I thought how flocks of tenners circled each wing.
There were pink official forms I wouldn't fill in

'this lad sells weed, cut scag, twists of crack...'
as most of what I'd learnt wasn't up for grabs

like: 'this "model" con is lying to me again...'
'this pal's stories are what he'd do to women...'

'this man is crow meat beneath the gantry stairs...'
'this big guy beats inmates in his care...'

Alim was a shade against the window's grille,
his hungry fingers rolling loose tobacco,

training his lighter with a nonchalant flick
as if to ask me 'what the fuck

do you know of trade?' He extended
a hand ('mate'), then turned back into the traffic of men.

\*

The day Alim asked me to bring a package in
a sleet-wind chased its tail behind the prison.

Louise, he said, would meet me in Forest Fields
(I pictured the snow-trim on her boots and furs,

the cold, pale colour of her eyes,
her slender fingers cradling the merchandise.)

I'd bear the parcel one dead afternoon
for its contents to be thinned and spooned

and wrapped – the stuff blowing out to smoke,
to dust lining toilets' clogged-up throats,

or this fine mist over the pool table's baize;
drifts to fleck sick-beds and guards' dark sleeves.

Alim hailed men who ambled from the showers –
towels round midriffs, tight muscles and tattoos –

tasty perhaps with blades in their hands.
If Alim owed some gang his days were contraband.

'I need to call some friends so stay in touch.
Louise wants to meet you very much.'

\*


No talk of cargo next time I saw him
what with the muster of thick-skinned policemen,

punters in cheap suits ranged for the Defence.
Alim propped his brush against the fence.

'I want to forget, when this trial collapses,
low-light and locks, shitty pillows and mattresses,

this taste of sweat that sours everything.
No more wind-blown sobs or midnight hymns,

men in the dead hours screaming cold turkey
or small voice that sings *I hate poetry*.'

He backed towards the wing. 'All I'll need,
when I chip it, is a teenth of good weed,

and swirling ice cubes in a noisy bar, Louise
who'll line up vodka, mobile, car keys.'

\*

I called a week later to ask if all was well:
a large bloke with a stammer filled the cell.

Alim had talked of a letter but his words were gone
the way of prison yard cherry blossom.

I weighed my chances of catching him in town
ghosted in a shop front, rain-dogged, head down

or grazing past him on the steps to the station:
an arm around her waist, stopping for no-one.

# Cells (i)

The ultrasound gleans
rib-light and coral fingers;
your heart a quick fish.


Dewfall, a morning
of webs quivering clotheslines:
late summer longhand.


Swifts shape a fly-by,
their high, riotous piercings,
and one year's shot past.

# Miniatures

*for Simon and Anna*

(i)

Just before you give in to sleep
I think how, in the dimness, you'll speak
to me in riddles, or rehearse
to the clock-face soft non-sequiturs,

but your questions without answers
are harder than the stars
whose failing signals dust our room...
*You promise me? How long now? Was it the moon?*

(ii)

Away from the cooker's hearth of steam
mum cradles Joseph for two stolen minutes
in the quiet attic room.
She holds the boy snug against her hip
swaying to tunes recalled from late-night feeds
when the house shed scents like a dark-petalled flower,
and the lightest curtains breathed out
and in toward a still hour.
Mum hands our boy back fast asleep
and returns to the kitchen's mist of flavours.

(iii)

You barely remember those first three months
but now each day's all memory
since you map his skin's spray of freckles
and watch his blond hairs blow auburn.

Already a first language has been lost
as the coastline of his ears unfolds,
and those milk-sweet stools that flecked your days
leave you like the smell of gloves from fingers.

Today the watermarks of his nipples,
the knuckle-buds and dimples of his fists:
you learn his body's tender reaches
just as he out-leaps you again.

(iv)

We curve left into an ambush of trees
surprised by saplings ranged along the verge
then trunks and branches thinning to infinity,
all laid out, pared back, manicured,
so much that light and bough-shade throw a pattern
as even as the fine weave of a rug.
Leaves stir like butterflies trembling in sun.
We smell green skins still buried in the wood.

I wonder if you'll remember how we cleave
the orchard, or stow this salt-wind's promise
of sea as we swing across the estuary
pointing at tractors, pigeon-whirr, this white horse
in a field?  What reflection holds you as we make
the bay and glimpse an ocean jinked with waves?

(v)

You call along our ginnel to catch its echo
the way you caw at rooftop crows
or blow my arm to try the sound of skin,
or slap your hands against this mossy wall.
Vowels fan out like petals around you.

(vi)

When I hear my dad's voice rise mid-song
over candle smut and pews
I wonder at my unlatched tongue
testing the way a low note circles
from bricks and timbers
then back inside my breath

where it wavers on updrafts
of sun-freckled dust; rests
like a butterfly on coloured glass.

(vii)

When you arrive to take him home
he's hunched over an ice field
of jigsaw pieces, palms puzzled with seals,
a bear's craw and tail flukes lashing foam,
his aim somewhere in the middle distance
where unerringly it snows perfect flakes
and a lone explorer hails the maker
of this blue sky's fragile brilliance.
You disturb him into words: *see jigsaw*,
so you bend to slowly melding floes,
and this dazzling craze of snow
stacked in drifts across the floor.
He's set on bergs and creaking sea;
you try to keep up, stumbling, knee-deep.

(viii)

Your Acer blows red kisses at the window.
We lunge into the teeth of the wind
to catch skittering leaves, whirl our arms
in the air, tease off glass – small as your palm –
flakes darkened almost to transparency.
You hold out colours that burn my hands –
oranges, crimsons, jagged pinks,
leaving prickles of frost on my fingers.
When we huddle through the fiercest gusts
your heartbeat flaps across my chest.

(ix)

We come on those born sleeping by the gates,
gravestones tended by solitary dates
dressed with stuck-eyed dolls, tissue frills
for flowers, a paper windmill
I let you spin until it purrs,
before we seek out butterflies and spiders.

(x)

Loosed on Barley Cove sands
he scrambles with gold dust for hands
like those hatchling turtles
that tunnel out, and pull beyond gulls.

He's clumsy-fierce, turns back
at each wave's soft crash,
bends with frittering shingle in range
to fix a fine moustache of grains.

When I lift him he wriggles
about my hip, big eyes bottles swilled
with light, and presses me to pick
salt-wind off his fingertips.

I hang on if I can
as he summons the ocean.

# Recapitulation Theory

surmises we begin as fish
then wriggle out with features like a frog's,
a lizard's, before the mammal in us surfaces.

These creatures sniff the air for something,
clawing at the light that keeps them pinned,
a lost terrain contoured on their skin.

They've burrowed up from deep inside our heads,
a swerve we cannot shake. We ask
of them the hardest things: to feel, to speak.

# Death and the Gallant

*for Susan Hatton*

**XXIII.** Also, that they shall take away, utterly extinct, and destroy all shrines, coverings of shrines, all tables, candlesticks, trindals, and rolls of wax, pictures, paintings, and all other monuments of feigned miracles, pilgrimages, idolatry, and superstition, so that there remain no memory of the same in walls, glass windows, or elsewhere within their churches and houses; preserving nevertheless, or repairing both the walls and glass windows; and they shall exhort all their parishioners to do the like within their several houses.

From *The Royal Injunctions of 1559*

**26.** UFFORD, JAN. the 27th. We brake down 30 superstitious Pictures; and gave direction to take down 37 more; and 40 Cherubims to be taken down of Wood; and the chancel levelled. There was a Picture of Christ on the Cross, and God the Father above it; and left 37 superstitious Pictures to be taken down; and took up 6 superstitious Inscriptions in Brass.

**27.** WOODBRIDGE, JAN. the 27th. We took down 2 superstitious Inscriptions in Brass; and gave order to take down 30 superstitious Pictures.

**28.** KESGRAVE, JAN. the 27th. We took down 6 superstitious Pictures; and gave order to take down 18 Cherubims, and to levell the Chancel.

**29.** RUSHMERE, JAN. the 27th. We brake down the Pictures of the 7 deadly Sins, and the Holy Lamb with a Cross about it; and 15 other superstitious Pictures.

**30.** CHATSHAM, JAN. the 29th. Nothing to be done.

**31.** WASHBROOK, JAN. the 29th. I broke down 26 superstitious Pictures; and gave order to take down a stoneing Cross and the Chancel to be levelled.

From *The Journal of William Dowsing, of Stratford*
*(Demolishing the Superstitious Pictures and Ornaments of Churches*
*within the County of Suffolk, in the Years 1643-1644)*

## I *The Adoration of the Magi*


Drove road to Saint Botolph's; psalms of wind
sound the tree-tops.  None to meet us
when we wade the flooded meadows of the parish,
then come dripping through the orchard.
Brown hangs his boots and shirt about the porch.
We have a scout.  Here are four wooden crosses,
stones that whisper *Ora pro nobis*,
star-breasted angels, and high above a northern arch

slow Magi loom from out the night.
Jasper's fit for fields more than a palace;
he kneels with gold that flares like tips of wheat,
his bare head touched by sun, grace, solace.
I fetch a ladder.  Brown works the whitewash,
and just for good measure, cuts Mary's face.

## II *A Reckoning*

I doze through storms in a godly farmer's barn
while Brown lies coddled in his mistress's bed.
I shouldn't bemoan my hard and dusty stead
but when Brown crows in the grey light of dawn
*More haste, old man,* I've ached less of mornings.
A seven-mile trudge under skies of lead
toward a spire craning high above the woods
like a heron eyeing a poppled stream.

More reckoning – swift effacement and flames –
as if what's blighted can be razed outright
and yet my wife is fourteen years a shade,
my five children I hold to my left-hand side
though to give each girl a name and age
would mean to clear the long grass from the grave.

## III *The Crucifixion*

Saint Anne's. The Passion on a southern wall.
When Nicodemus hefts his body down
this artist shows by Christ's pulled arms
the frame is slight yet burden's all.
As Brown stirs water into pails of chalk
I trail my shadow round this Lord's demesne –
closed cottages, forge, tavern, farm –
to root out screens made scarce and shrouded panels.

I've dug up roods like briars from a ditch,
once found a Christopher standing in a yard.
Doused in this wheat-ears' ruby light
I absolve my eyes from searching hard.
I turn a bottle's murky shine, then lift
it high to pledge my disregard.

IV *The Doom or Last Judgment*


Solemn over this chancel arch the Doom.
On this side, Peter lifts an arm to collect
a swim of souls, like silver from a net.
Beneath, the dead clamber from narrow tombs.
I point at sinister and say to Brown
*there's ones like you, stewing in sex...*
But Hell's not prised for Brown's gathered elect.
*And you, old man, do you rise or go down?*

Snow falls on fire.  Saved and damned lie buried
under snow.  Christ and his colours
under drifts of snow.  A frost will crust this nave
for stone years, bone years, well-deep years.
Now that Brown's gained a horse he'll bolt ahead
while I ruminate under the shattered stars.

## V *Saint James the Great*

Brown won't abide it but we're pilgrims too.
James, brass-limbed, bestride a transept wall
bears a low-slung pouch, yellow scallop shell,
his outstretched staff a warship's prow.
Brown the supplicant, could he bend so low,
would hear the North Atlantic's swell
against those flame-rigged citadels
and whisper prayers to this *Matamoros.*

He knows I see him check his hand
so has me daub out heraldry,
the face, the heart, then holy land.
Noon-wise, I find him supine under trees
clasping tied-up inventories and plans
like a sullen knight in effigy.

## VI *The Tree of Jesse*

More rain to fill the butts and troughs
as gargoyles spew forth sermons on the flood.
While Brown turns stables out for buried goods
I scale the Jesse tree before it's cut
and keep an aerie in its ample boughs.
A priest's dragged in with cries about a rood,
Brown's right arm tight around his head.
He's moved against the stone-carved font

and this man's christened with streams of blood,
a veil of crimson down his goggling face.
Now Brown will haul him from the muddy road
to the recusant Lord's estate
so that he might be understood.
This will teach us to hide our faith.

VII  *The Last Supper*


*Are you drunk again, old man?*
*Look up* I say, *none want for wine but Judas,*
but Brown no longer sees the pictures.
*Slacken from work and I'll mark your skin.*
So flesh too is made a painting
where one reads things base or superstitious,
my wrist a cut from being dangerous.
Brown would brand me among the damned.

Here's forty strokes to flay a painter's hand,
strike comely flesh back into chalk-white bone.
Christ's little nest of fingers won't withstand
the guest who's given silver and breaks his home.
His eyes, his azure eyes I blind,
his skin I mark outright, and so I'm done.

## VIII *Death and the Gallant*

I wake thick dust as chapel-sunlight pales
and into silence lift my stubborn breath.
Here's a courtier touched by wanton Death:
look how Thin-Bones jigs along the aisle,
fingers teasing up a dusky rose.
For our dandy turned by this address
how ill-judged his hat and boots and lacy cuffs
since he'll be fucked by a smirking corpse.

Brown has spies along these ferny roads.
I know he wants me dancing from a rope.
I will inter my sketchbook and my beads,
stow what bread I can procure about my coat,
and pick a trail over these moonlit fields.
What ghost disturbs my dark but my old love.

## IX *Spirits*

The woods are free with spirits, faeries, elves:
they moth my thoughts now dawn makes light of me.
I bless my boots to find such company
plagued as sprites are to bide amongst themselves
in dank and dappled corners of the realm.
Look how few they have become, how airy
under oak sway, waning almost to memory.
We listen.  For miles downwind the clamour of bells.

Brown lies close in some burgher's dainty house,
a knife and Bible set beside his bed.
Blessed the man who wakens to a chorus,
to panes of green and gold on a stream's rapt flood;
hails sky's thick blossom on high-domed boughs
even if his gentle friends have flown or fled.

## X *A Reckoning*

Best fight your wars on boggy fields.
As Brown halloos me by a brimming ditch
I come out carrying a hefty stick
to walk secure, to have a block to wield.
Brown moves like fire through the blighted wheat
but when he swings his blade the hot-head slips.
I stand, pivot, meet him with a kick
then club about his body and close-cropped head.

No pardon or last words: I cut him good.
He knows the journey of his immortal soul.
I drag then bury him deep inside the wood
and push a branch to crest the mud-filled hole.
I've breath enough to make my peace with God
then pray that Brown be delivered from hell.

# Cells (ii)

News of the virus
blew eastwards as starlings swerved
and shimmered at dusk.


We lived on berries,
rabbits, thaw-water, the month
of the explosions.


Last correspondence:
three pitted, friable scabs
in see-through packets.

## 'Now, now is the perfect time of my life'

O to be seventeen again
when all my autumn Saturdays
cast this edifice of rain;
when we loped between the bar and baize
of some half-empty basement lounge;
later striking out with mates
beyond the dark parades of town:
past flats, grand houses, to new estates,
in search of vinyl's carried bass.
Most nights we'd make the party list
by hailing nigh-on friendly faces:
school peers, sports buddies, brothers, sisters,
then worked a corner, settled in,
split our kitchen-pilfered tins.

One time I met this girl who said
'So you're a *serious* poet,
maybe…' – though she hadn't read
a jot, a breath of what I wrote –
'…your work befits that scold of Plath's,
you know: *these poems do not live,*
all drifting feet and dead-eyed craft,
*they sit so nicely in pickling fluid!*
The party boomed.  Kat showed her wrists,
the frailest, thinnest chat-up lines
I'd been presented with.  We kissed
among the trash and smears of wine;
that heady scent of sweet perfume.
My coat was hers: I walked her home.

Plath steered her diary entries through
'the rapture of being seventeen'.
Beyond the art above the bureau,
the chair and desk, the quiet trees…
'Always I want to be an observer.'
Yet here are thoughts she needs to say:
'I am afraid of getting older…
spare me from cooking three meals a day'.
I fixed a time to meet with Kat
but for one or untold reasons
watched my cloudy pint go flat.
We met the one time, post-exams,
an all-night bash; she wondered if
I still composed that schoolboy stuff.

Kat, I hope you're understood,
grown calm with blond-haired sons and daughters;
stashed about your townhouse study,
a dust-filmed, bleached-out *Crossing the Water*.
My lad-of-letters front, my lack
of gab or nous, my crap attempts
at holding all that spilt beer back,
I view now through the thickest lens.
A party shakes a neighbour's house
but even as I lie awake
and listen through the whoops and shouts
above a rough, insistent bass,
what jags and stirs the early hours –
my babies floating in their jars.

# Jigs and Reels

*i.m. John Maher*

# Thistledown / Cottongrass

The sonographer makes a sweep
for kicks, though you're convinced that dark
unravels light; you *feel* the beat
has ghosted from this three month heart.

I grip your hand and think of skin
more delicate than thistledown.
What floats and snags and drifts downwind
moons luminous with ultrasound.

Beyond, the city cambers east
as though its spires and tipped-up parks,
its messy diagram of streets,
all slip toward vanishing points.

The sonographer folds the snaps,
bins paper towels, then pitched between
practiced solicitude and tact
asks do we want to see the screen?

We stray wide over Beeley Moor
to mark my way at forty years
knee-high amongst the heather's cure
and cottongrass's tousled flares.

For two small dawdling boys you draw
these flits of bubbles on the breeze
that pink and kiss a dry stone wall
and take the grip of blackthorn trees,

or lift clear like a diver's breath,
so hikers watching from the rise
would see four solitary specks
stare at unassuming sky

and not suppose what holds them there
is light that quivers out of view
nor intimate the vista shared
is all the untold names for blue.

# A Journey Home / The Last Day of the Year

For William, hefted by a car
then stretched like breath along the curb:
my wound-up boy ran out so far
he missed the driver's throttled swerve.

He doubled up and dropped his words
because the hurt, this black surprise
had shot the orbit of his world,
a meteorite smacking ice.

In A&E I stroked his face
as though to draw his bruised-blue cheek
back to bone: my thumbs dabbed lips,
sure my touch would tease out speech.

Yet Billy, barrelling, robust,
a week on tugged free from my arm
to rush a noisy road on trust
wanting words for care or harm.

To last till midnight, sleep an hour
and lose this fogbound afternoon;
to draw in, braid the breath you share,
and slow a dusk-encumbered room.

Your kids doze close with coupled fists
as though they cradle loops of rope
that tether backs to knees to hips
like four bound sailors in a boat.

Press here: heel-kicks against your palm
flash life like starlight marking time:
you feel a universe of harm
imperceptibly realign.

Tonight's New Year. The weatherman
forecasts a bone-cold ten below,
but now you cling to heat and skin
to banish auguries of snow.

# 3 a.m. / Kiss the Baby

Our boy's pulled blue and wetly coiled
into the world, and all is cries.
Once you've been stitched and dressed and wheeled
down to the ward, I kiss goodbye,

a spaceman angling for the moon.
Adrift, this hour I blink in light
on corridors by curtained rooms
with thoughts that arc the rim of night.

These doors are shut.  Sleepover cars
glow orange under cauls of frost:
an inch away from cool night air
I'm high, dog-tired, near home and lost

and now, to track up bleach-white steps
past stirs and whispers on the wing
where you tend to hothouse breaths,
I'll never touch this star again.

Always time to kiss the baby,
cradled chest-high, laying down;
off to work each day a pay-day;
bless late hours without a sound.

Always time round café tables,
parties, picnics, dappled walks;
stopped out shopping by a lady
who clucks and, kissing cheeks, sweet talks.

Maureen calling from the kitchen,
stretchered to the ambulance;
another stroke, her heartbeat thickened,
blankets ravelled through her hands,

though she's time to halt her train
and hail us while we stand there, waving,
certain we'll see her home again;
lifts herself to kiss the baby.

# Angry Woman / Running Woman

*Two George Fullard Sculptures, Upper Chapel, Sheffield*


I hear her cries then see her gyre
beside the awning-darkened bar,
and though it pours she sparks with fire
the way her buckled fingers claw.

Sometimes her body finds its place
loose inside this ruckled dress
but from her shucked and washed-out face
slips this closely borne confession:

*He chatted sweet in Fagan's snug*
*and bought me halves of blackout-stout.*
*We danced a slow dance round the pub;*
*past closing time he took me out*

*then threw me hard against a wall,*
*pulled and wrestled back my arms.*
*I jerked and kneed him in the balls*
*for all his claims he meant no harm.*

First the searchlights, then the thunder.
A woman bolts across the square:
high-stacked heels, stole-folded shoulders,
raindrop earrings, slicked-back hair.

To sketch her now: thin knees and elbows
ridge a pleated, velvet gown.
I have her nose as beaky shelf:
a crow that clatters midnight boughs.

I sculpt her hurtling from alarm
in casts that gauge the clipping gait
of one who's tripped and braced by time.
For running always: always late.

Glance backwards: bombs begin to fall
like flowers sent to pin her hair,
but she's street-lengths beyond recall;
her tail of perfume blown to air.

# Hurdy-Gurdy / Late Note

The times I've been marooned in snugs
with pint in hand, or fluked a lock-in
by dint of some backwater pub
hosting fiddlers, strummers, box-men,

hale singers, hurdy-gurdy players,
your oboe's curlicue of notes… and gifted
all my fusty words away
for companionship like this,

to drive a tune that bumps and slides
across the flags like chords on castors;
ride the pick, the wheeze, the grind
of this reel-out-rolling craft,

my shoulder to the rhythm's weight,
brace, let go a jig or song
that trips and changes on the beat,
nailed down, thrown off, rattled on

Becomes our house silenced by tunes
the hour you play your oboe late:
scales concatenating rooms,
blank windows, dormers starred by notes.

Each air you've scribed or learnt by ear,
a schottische, polka, easy waltz,
trips off its steps to find me here
relearning half-remembered holds.

You're charmed beneath a lamp's full moon,
why else draw circles with the bell
and through that concentrated frown
pull long silver from a well?

You're spread-legged, centred, pitched in rhymes,
have much of everything by heart,
and for the moment beat out time.
You stop to catch my gaze, and start.

# A Basque Blues / Desert Song


Alarde Hondarribia!
Now bereted menfolk hammer town
with pipes and tambours; sip cold beer,
still facing Bourbon cannons down.

But youths who file in hoops of noise
have Civil Guards to hem them in,
their gazes fierce as girls' and boys'
on bills round San Sebastian.

For all the chants and hoots to drums,
flags and banners, fists held high,
the show is soldiers cradling guns
in ski masks Zapatista-style.

The kids are jostled off the march.
The bands keep time even as rain
blackens rooftops, bangs, discharges
the tail-end of a hurricane.

One dust patrol you found a bed,
beached like drift across some street,
and perched on heaps of clothes this head
already at its winding sheet.

The time it took to lift your sights
this guy had caught your stink and woke
and flung arms wide to shore up night,
dug 'don't shoot' from out his throat.

You watched him scoot.  What's one more man
fetching up on hands and knees
to retch his weight in blood on sand,
drowning outwards by degrees.

You checked the mattress: shawls and burkas,
cotton pants and children's shirts,
thought who'd want this pile of hurt –
shoes, those sweats with stitched-on words.

# A Conversation / For the Lad

At a poet's birthday bash
I met him shadowing the bar,
this big man with the finest lashes
who touched upon his 'slim career'.

Two books.  I'd read them, yakked about
his gift of letting readers in:
a generous opening out,
his crafted lack of possession.

This poem's edge of prickly scent,
that close attention to her skin,
its blush and fade to transparency,
outspread a tender offering.

He shrugged it off and took his drink.
I say this since he's three years dead,
his scripts undone, or out of print,
and want him here still: writing, read.

I mark the lad who flunked my class
because he failed to show his face,
though studied snug and tap house brass,
the clubs, beer gardens, small cafés,

and once because he took some stuff
that let him fray apart one night,
it picked the stitching from his breath
then slurred his blood, and stopped his heart.

I chip these quatrain blocks in part
to show precisely what he's missed
though understand the end of art
both magnifies, diminishes.

So what I wish to tell this kid
who's left to lie all afternoon
among his drafts, his books of lit.
is *class begins now, wake up son.*

# Bristle / Blemish

My dad once groomed a fat moustache,
I've gleaned this from a single snap:
he's twenty-some, boyish, relaxed,
styled hair, pale turtleneck, a tache.

I bend to light to glimpse a man
who threads his lip for – count them – weeks
because thus far in life he can,
and isn't set, restrained, discreet;

isn't quite the face I find:
the spread, those wrinkles, flattened strands,
and more, what shaving leaves behind –
this distillation of the man.

So what if once he trimmed a line?
Silvered, stubble-faced, I move
to hold his head just out of time
before his bristle's splashed round, sluiced.

First light: today our youngest's one,
and since he's crooked my arm all year
I cup his head toward the sun
to sift his tufts and flicks of hair

for rufous, auburn, curls turned fair,
the brown then red tinge of his lashes,
this pinch of fur around his ears
and copper brows as fine as foxes.

Each iris floats in its own shine;
here's blue surprised by freckling gold
and blue-green graduated lines.
His eyes adjust to see me whole,

and we gaze back at all our sum
of spots and veins, each bump and blemish,
each chestnut mole I touch to number
that marks the forty years between us.

# Movies

There are films I've never lasted through,
late night flicks, or my boys' favourite movies:
pics chosen on days of hurrying rain;
some toon between breakfast and soccer training;
puff-eyed popcorn matinees of sprawl
where I catch my kids' almost perfect recall.

Aimed toward the edge of things most days
I must have watched these films backward, sideways
pausing in the light-trap of the hall
or as chaperone to check the spats and brawls;
have vied for sofa-room on breaks from work
to hang a storyline on odd excerpts.

Out of darkness other close-ups flicker:
a bottle pressed to my son's dry lips,
how he heeds the screen in spite of fever;
a child I couch along my sleeve,
too small to focus on the blue-red strobe
that gives his head the faintest glow.

The four of us knee-deep among the cushions
move from chat toward a moment's hush,
caught out by plot, by love, some tricky part,
and though I try to learn these scenes by heart
I'm lost for words, distracted – see, I'm crying
and when you ask me I can't tell you why.

# Shake

When we drag up bedclothes off the floor
to stow this heat from breasts and limbs,
I pull as though we're hauling nets onshore
so full the weight against our freckled skins,
so shook this salt-and-silver dark…
and stillness coming on, a tipping point
that takes us like the slowing of the heart,
the ache that sifts through all these tender joints.

Now, around this lull, I feel you shake
the way that grief drives in like rain at sea.
Against my arm you've turned your face,
because I think these kisses make you weep:
your open side's all tangled up with pain
yet who am I to rock you back
given where you're aimed is out of range
and all the words I have can't speak your lack.

# Wicker

Fed with gold you dream
of sandbanks, sunspots, finches.
Your blood silts up with light,
heart glitters metal traces.
Weighed, your body is precious.


Buoyed on these midstream
popples, I dream an otter.
Its head is a nib
writing light, throat quicksilver.
Whiskers bristle out winter.


Squat, green bulbs, bitter
as smoke, I offer you figs
from Sheffield's east end.
They have exile's toughened flesh
and skin; its deep-cut bloodline.

# King of Rock 'n' Roll

I came on Paddy by Eldon Square,
oblique, conspicuous in thick-lensed frames,
raking back his straggly hair,
fame-shy and waiting for what fame

might come – this was between the *Steve McQueen*
and *Memphis* albums – a steer from tunes
left dreaming lights beyond the Tyne,
to tracks that promised penthouse views.

I was eighteen and awkward as elbows.
Paddy had this frail mystique
as artist of a chrome-mooned Great North Road,
safe on the high wire of his lyric

as the guy who shunned all stir and buzz
beneath the tender stitch-work of each song;
fragile as star-shine for seeming like us,
who soon as I caught wind of was gone.

# The Reading

When Ken arrives his foot's encased in plaster;
he wheels this trolley like a gentle curse,
though shrugs off pain before I've time to ask

what turned him lame: concern would make it worse;
*a bloody stupid thing* is all he says.
A short walk later Ken is nursing

a pint, while we as hosts assert, rephrase
the woes of modern verse, but with the drink
and our cross-talk the rattle level's raised:

*Shut up*, he growls, *I can't hear myself think.*
A friend will joke about unpeeling his moustache
as if another Ken hides underneath

but propped outside he scoffs his fish with gusto,
and when he reads, his weighed voice never wavers.
Our bloody-minded poet won't be rushed –

will muse on hats in every flavour
for ten whole minutes; pausing once to burp
his chip shop apologia.

Post-reading, Ken looks pummelled from his work,
but still has form to join us in The Grapes,
bearing books, reserve, the leg that *doesn't* hurt.

'Ken.' *What?* 'Ken.' *Yes?* Though questions now escape me,
I'll remedy what I should have said:
a view that keeps you restless, the way you face

this keening wind, how you mark the edges,
leaves you peerless; don't slow down, don't settle,
don't at sixty-four, Ken, end up dead.

# An Invitation

A taxi – Chinatown to Haight –
compels my Polish guide to state
as we crisscross the grid of streets
'Your Chinese worker never sleeps.'
He asks what's pushed me out this way,
this wet September on the bay,
an Englishman with scripts and notes,
a quill of Post-its scrawled with quotes:
I'm here, I say, to meet Thom Gunn,
poet, expat, citizen.

Thom shows me round his airy home
of lacquered timbers banked with tomes,
a spruce, clean-cut civility
like light that shelves in from the sea.
He's easy, bear-like, big with charm,
blue jeans, black panther on his arm,
an earring glints; he talks and flirts
though when I err he smooths his shirt,
in no uncertain terms explains
he never trekked to Fascist Spain.

I ask him stuff he's heard before
because I'm thrown, unversed, in awe,
and Thom has ample grace to chart
rehearsed accounts around his art.
The private man has stepped outside
to read, swill beer, go hitch a ride,
and left this version of himself
that's learned, playful, lacking stealth.
I ask him things he doesn't know:
'I wrote that forty years ago!'

When Mike returns with bags and books
he greets me with a wary look:
*another lettered boy who's come*
*to worship at the feet of Gunn.*
I guess my motives are a given
except I keep some knowledge hidden –
asked to quiz, not explicate,
what need have I to say I'm straight?
I stop the tape – on little reels
this roughed out, done and dusted deal.

Unfazed by what or who I am,
Thom walks me down to catch the tram,
a kindly host until the end
– 'Hey, August!' greets a writer friend –
he shows me how to sort the fare:
'A dollar gets you anywhere'.
He's bigger now he shakes my hand,
grows larger, gains, from where I stand:
I watch him turn and saunter home,
a streetwise dude from some old poem.

# Every Time We Met

## 1

'Good health.'  He lifts a muddy beer.
'Christ, it must be two or three…'
I clarify: 'It's been *four* years.
Bristol.  I came to hear you read
at that conference on form and verse,
when Daniel Stoddard had a pop
at you for words, a snub, a slur.
Before he swung I dragged you off.
We took a time-out, walked the grounds,
then justified not being missed
by trawling pubs that fringed the Downs,
ended high up on the bridge.'
'Of course', he raises hands to bless
and wave off talk of waywardness.

'So when's this tome on me appearing?'
'Once the text's been polished, proofed,
I'm hoping maybe spring next year.
But Greg, it's *chapters* of a book.
I'm here to check my facts are right
though mostly want to pick your brain
on why early in your writing life
you hit a rich creative vein?'
He throws the look he aimed at me
twenty years ago or more
when we exchanged brief pleasantries
across a Gents' wet-tiled floor.
I saw him first read in a pub,
the boy made good back from Oxford,

crossed him later pissing gold;
said I thought his work impressive –
one of the best new poets I'd heard.
'Thanks.' Then that look: *one of the best!*
Somehow his face has travelled south,
hence that looseness round his chin,
the puffed and pinched, pull-rip-cord mouth,
sunned but punctuated skin.
For all his fixed and whitened teeth,
work done on his thinning hair
and everything concealed beneath,
his features have a lived-in air
and Time's called round its pals in truth.
I talked too much, a callow youth.

'Okay, once I've sunk this pint
we'll head back home so you can ask
whatever bloody thing you like
about my uneventful past.
But tell me, Ed, do you still *write?*'
'The longhand stuff, the poems, no –
despite the brief acclaim, the prize,
I lost momentum years ago.'
'The cheque we shared in ninety-five?
Post the judges' endless questions
didn't we find some chi-chi dive
off a boulevard in Kensington?'
That first award was ninety-six
though I don't pull him up on this

or say now what I doubtless knew
even when I garnered praise:
*I'll never write as well as you.*
These things dig in from that day:
the heat and haze, that sticky mix
of car fumes, flowers, an oily sweat
like nowhere else, the taste of bricks;
then Gregory's *Ars Poetica*
perfected over fags and ale
which disavowed the singing heart
for pushing words around a page;
and lastly, click-clack through the bar
Leigh wearing that wrap-around skirt;
anklet, sling-backs, tie-dye shirt.

'I don't recall the bar's allure.
But bagging prizes must've, well,
forgive the cliché, opened doors.'
'Any artist who has work to sell
should seek to optimize his take:
me, I'd shoulder-barge a wall
if bruises led to sure-fire breaks.
Success is not a tricky call',
Greg swills the ruff that lips his beer,
'we love its *weight*, crave readers, patrons,
inveigle tributes from our peers –
I mean this book that you are shaping,
all your kick-ass style and wit's
in part to clinch a Professorship?

Yes, I got published then got tenure,
teaching bright kids how to rhyme
on the west coast of America
thinking even my shit would shine,
but dried up chewing college tit.
And Leigh soon tired of making art
on land she'd no connection with
so we came home: old life, new start.'
I know this snatch of story arc
since Greg gave over four cold months
to renting in the National Park;
I met him twice in town for lunch
once with Leigh and once alone,
a man already come and gone.

That second meeting's worth relating
as Greg seemed less than bulletproof,
I mean his views, assertions, statements,
stayed in the ballpark of the truth.
More, he edged so close to doubt,
whispered smoke hung like a mask
that coloured half his face in cloud,
his airy guard all but collapsed.
I guess he wanted secrets buried
a little distance shy of home,
intuited I could be trusted
with stuff he labelled 'burdensome',
mine being the closest ear
to load before he disappeared.

Said the point of coming back
was tied up with this other girl
he'd met just once though stayed in contact
while schlepping through collegiate 'hell'.
He wrote her, odd times phoned her late;
cultivated a 'formal' tone.
He scrawled her poems for goodness sake!
Leigh's main aim returning home
that urge to overhaul her art,
meant she spared him little time
so couldn't sense things fall apart.
He was about to take a ride…
Greg bangs his glass down: 'C'mon, let's go.
I need some air.  I need a smoke.'


I didn't speak to Greg again
until the Bristol tête-à-tête.
For sure, we emailed now and then;
a text blew in like desert sleet
(*thx for your reviews*) and once I waved
at him across a London street.
Lost inside that long decade
were hotels where we almost met.
The heat then scents of this June night:
we skirt the car park's four by fours,
trip the barley-coloured lights
that obfuscate all sign of stars,
then find the lane; Greg's tip of ash
an only lamp, his lone dispatch.

2

'Is Stoddard in this book of yours?'
We pause outside Greg's fenced-off land.
'Dan gets a look in – yes, of course.'
'What *could* you write about that man?
Well, one – his style's all lip and fists.
You saw that when he lost the plot.
And two – he's judged a plagiarist
by guys whose views I trust a lot.'
*Dan got mad from catching sight*
*of your whispers-on-the-backstairs tryst*
*with a woman who was not your wife,*
*and took you for a hypocrite.*
I want to speak the things but choose
wide open silence: too much to lose.

Greg's wife is Leigh: he 'toughed it out'.
Tied the knot five years ago.
Listen, before we reach the house
there's other stuff you need to know.
I always thought Greg needed Leigh:
she was the one who held the room,
who cultivated company,
who was the kinder of the two.
When Leigh breezed through that London pub
and talked about her vandal art –
how she'd daub 'grand' landscapes to scrub
them out, hack canvases apart,
then archive brushstrokes, scrapes and blows
in clear and systematic prose –

it seemed the most effacing craft.
I touched on agents, dealers, patrons,
hustling sales, but she just laughed:
'I critique the artist's role as maker.'
And on returning from the States
with Greg in one almighty funk –
the day Leigh sipped her skinny latte
while Greg got double-barreled drunk –
at least she had the wit to ask
a touch about my post-Doc slog –
reviews, short papers, monograph –
to bag an arse-end teaching job,
though heard far more about the damage
following my car-crash marriage.

I found her quite by chance one time
ensconced in some beige coffee shop.
Greg, she said, was doing fine,
though took himself away a lot.
His absence gave her room to plan
new strategies to mend her art
'but well, you know', she waved her hand,
'who'd choose to live here for a start?'
'But you don't *live* here', I replied.
'You need to dust your notions down,
leave your books and go outside.
I could show you round this town.
Surely you're curious to look
around the streets where Greg grew up?'

Our rendezvous one cold week on:
parkland, swings trimmed out in snow.
We kept the brook toward Forge Dam
then cut clean prints for Ringinglow,
the city's silks a parachute
folded, stowed behind our backs;
ahead a crushed-white, dirty scoop
of dry stone walls and fields and tracks.
Drifts.  Snow-air on Higger Tor:
what was that comfort found between us
high above the valley floor
as we turned round on the rim of dusk?
I mean, what else dictates a walk
but sharing open rhythms, talk?

The thaw took hold before I phoned
to ask if I could see her art.
I made tracks to her rented home
a mile beyond the reservoir.
Leigh's studio, the attic space
was hung with densely patterned boards
that detailed plans all but erased.
Leigh showed me drafts for 'Higger Tor':
scratched through paints, a sketch crossed out,
tattered photographic prints: her text
a narrative of prospects lost.
And yes, you're right, we did have sex
among the trashed, the scored, and damaged,
held fast on a narrow bed.

After that, you'll have to whistle.
Within a month Leigh left with Greg.
For all the chat I will not spill
will not spell out every time we met.
Still, one day I spoke her name
to have her skin play on my lips
in a hotel room close by the Thames.
The OXO Tower's cherry kiss
slow bled in the tidal dusk
while we discussed a year mislaid,
regained ourselves, showered and dressed.
I shot the stairs, the lobby, made
the bank toward Blackfriars bridge
(all mauve fluorescent ribs)

for Greg to hail me cars away,
his smile right there across the street
and me all rubbed up, wet with spray.
I slowed to wave then picked up speed.
And this man I hadn't seen for years,
this man I'd cuckolded that hour
showed the face he offers me here
in this lamp's pale yellow shower
as we trail around the gable end;
a face with nailed-on cigarette,
hand plucking smoke, pinkie extended,
his eyes wee studies of reflection
rheumy from some magnified sense
of injury, entitlement.

A voice one midnight, distant, curt:
'Greg and I are getting married
and since I aim to make this work
this is goodbye. I'm sorry. Sorry.'
I spoke her name. The line went dead.
How to speak the life that's hidden?
There was no invite to the wedding.
I am a guest here and unbidden.
That Greg still saw the other woman
beyond the banquet and bouquets
was common knowledge all along
though what Leigh ever knew, who can say.
I never dropped the truth on Leigh.
She hardly broached home-life with me.

We linger on the creaky porch
like schoolboys thinking up some ruse.
Greg asks me if I'm happy, sorted.
'I've studied you for twenty years
and know you better than you know.'
This makes him smile, the omnivore
who eats the whole world in one go,
its soft, sweet flesh, the pips and core.
My mobile hums against my thigh
and for the third time in five days
I scan the same cursory style
in a text that riffs on *stay away*,
and for the third time in a week
I skim my thumb and press *delete*.

3

'Which artist saw your better self?'
'A birthday present from my wife.'
Greg broods above the mantel shelf
fleshed out with a palette knife.
'Leigh's come around to portraiture
now that she's junked the anti-art.
I mean who cultivates a future
carving boards and frames in half?
You've met my wife?' 'Yes, years ago.
Has Leigh gone AWOL for the night?'
'She's probably in her studio.'
He points out in the dark a light,
a glow worm of old wood and glass
hedged with blooms and waist-high grass.

His boots push at the table edge,
says: 'Okay, Edward, fire away.'
Makes his chair sit up and beg.
'The girl who lured you from the States,
the one who shared your other life
of trysts and scams and stolen kisses,
didn't she become Dan Stoddard's wife?'
He's thrown so much he almost tips.
'I don't see why you've mentioned this.'
'Perhaps when Dan saw Beth and you
sidling steps, all smiles and whispers,
and you gestured something pointed, lewd,
he had a right to feel aggrieved.'
'You know I think you'd better leave.'

'And Leigh, the heiress of reserve
focused on her perfect craft
what would she raze now if she heard
you screw around behind her back?'
He stands with a burnt man's grace,
shaking out those flabby arms
in readiness to smack my face,
so I rise to meet him, offer palms:
'Fine, I understand your need
to defend the Greg Ruffini brand
but what *gives* regarding you and Leigh
when she sees the marriage is a sham?'
I'm dust. Walk out. Desert the grounds.
Greg-all-mouth doesn't hunt me down.

I hang about the entrance gate.
Stillness. The slender scent of flowers,
a plane's high thunder while I wait
for almost, damn it, half an hour
before I take to trespassing.
Wise to lighting up the drive
I wade in through the wetting grass
that flanks the lawns on either side,
a cobble's throw beyond the house,
then follow tracks toward the meadow.
It's when I ford the watercourse
and smell the resins off the shed
I spy inside this shape, this shade.
As stupid as it sounds, I wave

then knock and wrest the door ajar.
Leigh's bent before a charcoal sketch
of trees and fields, a church and farm
about to brush an oily speck,
a blue and silver dab of light,
to conjure this bone-china sky.
'I thought of going out tonight
but hey', she turns, 'I'll bide my time
knee-deep in these pools of paint.
It's true, I've dreamt up slights and snubs
but as one of us should show restraint
I'm loath to cause you any trouble.
And why should I vacate my home
for shit that happened years ago?'

She aims toward me, shakes my hand,
her skin to touch all rough and tender.
'You', I tell her, 'weren't in my plans
until I spotted Greg again
in my home town not three weeks back,
hustling through the evening crowds
like *someone* with the sun to catch,
except he had a friend in tow.
And when I glimpsed your tied-back hair
I thought I'd come and say *how's tricks?*
but then I realized…' 'Stop right there',
Leigh cuts my breath off with a click,
'Why have you tracked me down to speak
of episodes not worth repeating?'

'Leigh, there's things we *need* to share.'
'Fine', she says, 'if urgency
accounts for why you've taken care
to disregard my texted pleas
then hoodwink Greg and break in here,
I want to know why the *one time*
when I *needed* you, you disappeared?
You're good at spinning out a line
yet even so, I still believed
you'd show outside the hospital
after late-night guarantees.
Deeper bonds? You lost it all
while I stuck around for your support
hugging bags by plate glass doors.'

'Leigh, we've been through this before.'
'Sure, Ed. I used to wreck my art.
You watched me hurl frames at the floor.
But then, one day, a change of heart;
I fashioned tiny woodland flowers.
I crafted views of hills and lakes
and mountain-shadowed panoramas.
I will not make the same mistakes.
You've skulked in here to set things straight
by twisting fingers on this hand.
You think I need an education
from just another selfish man?'
'Please, Leigh…' 'Don't start. Don't bleat or beg.
If you *keep on* I'm phoning Greg.'

I back away. 'Okay, I'll go.
You look exhausted. Get some kip.'
I set off through the undergrowth
hoiking brambles with a stick
until I reach the grassy verge
that opens onto beds and baize,
a view that regiments my urge
to swing the stick in artful ways.
It's then I spy Greg on his rounds
drawn like some lugubrious owl
to sweep the limits of his grounds.
He rests against a lime tree's bole
blowing smoke. A silhouette.
A flat man. How appropriate.

I keep to hedged-in, scented paths
that should just ghost me out of view
then edge the courtyard, don't look back
even when I hear 'Hey, you!'
thrown up like some cannonball
from near the misted swimming pool.
I could return to test his crawl,
list his bag of crimes in full
but opt instead to cut outside,
to spit, unzip, and thread an arc
across the tarmac of Greg's drive,
let it taint the fragrant dark.
For what it's worth, I send two texts:
*There was no book.*
*Her name is Beth.*

# Cells (iii)

I am stone clover,
trinity of light and air,
harrowing darkness.


Seed each cell with light
then tell how the brightest stars
are first to flare out.


Redwoods survive fires
the way we'd like to outlive
pain: old heart, new skin.

# Notes

**Sentences**
This poem, originally published in *Staple* 72, was shortlisted for The Forward Prize For Best Single Poem 2011.

**Cells**
The 'Cells' sequences (i-iii) are a collection of haiku drawn from a number of collaborative projects I undertook with other artists and poets over the past decade. In the original 'Cells' exhibition I worked with the artist Paul Evans, creating poems alongside a series of watercolours he had painted. The work was first shown at the Cupola Gallery, Sheffield, in autumn 2007, then at the 20-21 Visual Arts Centre in Scunthorpe and furthermore in the Origin010 exhibition at the SIA Gallery, Sheffield. Other haiku are collected from 'Call and Response' (http://callandresponsehaiku.wordpress.com) and from a collaboration with Paul Evans and the poet Matthew Clegg for the new Cancer Genetics Building in Cardiff. The poems and paintings were 'unveiled' at the opening of the facility in 2010.

**Miniatures** and **Jigs and Reels**
'Miniatures' was originally published as a limited edition pamphlet by Longbarrow Press in 2007. 'Jigs and Reels' appeared in a pamphlet of the same name (Shoestring Press, 2013) with 'Skin', '*Now, now* is the perfect time of my life', 'Movies', 'King of Rock 'n' Roll', 'The Reading' and 'An Invitation'.

**Recapitulation Theory**
This poem was written as a commission for the Alfred Denny Museum, University of Sheffield, in collaboration with the artist Paul Evans and the photographer Karl Hurst. The poem was also included in 'All Things Bright and Beautiful', an exhibition featuring various artists' work at 20-21 Visual Arts Centre, Scunthorpe in 2012-13.

**Death and the Gallant**

The extract of *The Journal of William Dowsing* I use here comes from a volume edited by the Rev C. H. Evelyn White (published in 1885). A full copy of Dowsing's text can be read online in various versions. My interest in Pre-Reformation wall painting came in part from Andrew Graham-Dixon's television series *A History of British Art* and his accompanying book (1996). The first chapter, 'Dreams and Hammers', offers an excellent introduction to ideas of iconoclasm and its effects on the British psyche. For a more academic overview of iconoclasm during the Reformation, see Eamon Duffy's *The Stripping of the Altars* (Yale University Press, 2005). Much of the information I use for *Death and the Gallant* comes from *Medieval Wall Paintings* by Roger Rosewell (The Boydell Press, 2008). Finally, an online resource I frequently visited was Paintedchurch.org. The site catalogues many examples of various Biblical (and religious) paintings, offering glimpses of how our medieval churches would have appeared to their congregations.


**The Reading**

I invited the English poet Ken Smith (1938-2003) to read in Sheffield in 1998. A good selection of his work can be found in *The Poet Reclining: Selected Poems 1962-1980* (Bloodaxe, 1982), and in *Shed: Poems 1980-2001* (Bloodaxe, 2002).


**Thanks**

I am grateful to the following readers who have helped me in the writing of these poems: Matthew Clegg, Gerard Curran, Paul Evans, Mark Goodwin, David Harmer, A.B. Jackson, Colin Jackson, John Lucas, Andrew Maddon, Felicity Skelton, David Swann, Rachael Weiss, Linda Lee Welch and Noel Williams. I would also like to thank Brian Lewis for his continual support and for his comments on the manuscript in the final stages of writing and redrafting.

Special thanks and love go to Jo, Joseph, William and Robert.